A Woman Like You

PRAISE FOR
A Woman Like You

"Vera Anderson's photos are haunting and hopeful, compelling in their message that violence can hit any family, any culture or ethnicity, any woman, well-off or poor. The stories and the faces of the women in this book are a beacon for all of us, a wake-up call, reminding us that violence will only end when all of us participate in ending it. And in bringing it together, Vera Anderson, as our documentarian and guide, takes us one step closer to a safer world."

> — *Sheila James Kuehl, Speaker pro Tem of the California State Assembly*

"The question is asked so often that it becomes tiresome: 'What kind of a woman would stay in a relationship with someone who abused her?' As Vera Anderson's portraits so eloquently document, the answer to that question is this: 'You. Me. Our daughters. Our mothers. Our grand-mothers.' The faces of these women, survivors all, are poignant reminders that the questions we ask are so often the wrong ones. Anderson's photographs demand we ask new questions: 'How can we put to rest the tired stereotypes about battered women? How can we persuade the world it could happen to anyone?' Look upon these portraits, and the powerful words that accompany them, as a way of doing that."

> — *Robin Abcarian*, Los Angeles Times

"Vera Anderson's book is a rare achievement providing artistic as well as cultural impact and significance. Anderson, who is a skilled photographer, utilizes her own experience of abuse, to help us see the range and complexity of the problem. The unique and personal views of her subjects add to the portraiture to help us see the issues from inside and out. [An] amazing book which goes a long way to removing stereotypes about abused women."

> — *Edward Wortz, Ph.D, psychologist, art collector and co-curator of* Addictions, *Santa Barbara Contemporary Arts Forum*

"Vera Anderson has created a compelling testament that spousal abuse can, and does happen to anyone. Most of all it provides a vehicle to break through the isolation of women. I hear the echo of my sister's voice in so many of these stories. I wish she had heard them so that she could have known she was not alone. Maybe then she might have left before it was too late."

— *Abby Leibman, Executive Director of the California Women's Law Center and sister of a woman who was killed by her husband*

"The eyes are the first and lasting powerful impression of photojournalist Vera Anderson's collection. They command attention, demand a response. It is time to face these eyes, these portraits Anderson puts before us. The truth they carry may be our first step in an urgent and necessary process of healing."

— *Rabbi Harvey J. Fields, Wilshire Boulevard Temple, Los Angeles*

A Woman
Like You

THE FACE OF DOMESTIC VIOLENCE

INTERVIEWS AND PHOTOGRAPHS BY

VERA ANDERSON

Seal Press
Seattle

Seal Press
3131 Western Avenue, Suite 410
Seattle, Washington 98121
sealprss@scn.org

Library of Congress Cataloging-in-Publication Data
Anderson, Vera
A woman like you : the face of domestic violence / interviews
and photographs by Vera Anderson (New Leaf Series)
Includes bibliographical references.
1. Family violence—United States. 2. Family violence—United
States—Pictorial works. 3. Victims of family violence—United States.
4. Victims of family violence—United States—Pictorial works. 5. Abused
women—Counseling of—United States. 6. Abused women—Counseling
of—United States—Pictorial works. I. Title.
HV6626.2.A53   1997   362.82'92'0973—dc21   97–22790
ISBN 1-878067-07-9

Printed in the United States of America
First printing, October 1997
1   3   5   7   9   10   8   6   4   2

Distributed to the trade by Publishers Group West
In Canada: Publishers Group West Canada, Toronto
In Europe and the U.K.: Airlift Book Company, London
In Australia: Banyan Tree Book Distributors, Kent Town

Cover design by Trina Stahl
Text design and composition by Rebecca Engrav
All photographs printed by Isgo Lepejian

With heartfelt thanks to:

Sheila James Kuehl, for opening the first door
Glenda Virgil, for letting me in
Gail Pincus, for her unparalleled dedication
Faith Conlon and Seal Press, for having the vision
Paul Duran, for his endless patience and support

and to all of my friends, and so many strangers, who in one
way or another helped this project stay alive, most notably:

Renee Williams
C.W.A.A. at C.I.W.
Karen Comegys
Susanne Filkins
Greg Canes at CNN
Joyce Winkler

and

Maggie, for her unconditional love,
her boundless spirit,
and her cold Scotty nose

For my daughter Emilie
my inspiration, my teacher, my friend

A Woman Like You

A woman is battered
in this country
every nine seconds.

Photo: Paul Duran

VERA ANDERSON

the interviewer/photographer

My husband and I were so much in love when we got married; the smart, talented, upwardly mobile, beautiful auburn couple. Jerry Harvey's dark side had attracted me in the beginning, the troubled genius with the sarcastic wit. I believed that we were different from other people, that I could help him, that loving him enough would ease his private demons. I didn't see my self-esteem being whittled away by the constant verbal abuse; I made excuses to myself for his behavior and I stayed in my marriage because I believed in my vows. No one knew; so intelligent and subliminal were his emotional manipulations that it was indiscernible to anyone on the outside looking in.

Seven years later, newly divorced from this man I loved after he terrorized me with a loaded gun, I was so emotionally paralyzed that I couldn't open my mail, literally collecting everything except utilities bills in a shoe box, unopened for over a year. I would erase messages on my answering machine without listening to them. I gained thirty pounds and did anything I could to anesthetize myself. My burgeoning photographic business dwindled. I could not identify or acknowledge the pain I felt. After all, I was smart, shouldn't I just be able to get on with my life? But I couldn't. Even after he remarried, he wouldn't leave me alone. It was as though I had this secret nightmare, sucking the very lifeblood out of me. When I tried to articulate what I felt, no one really listened. And certainly no one ever believed I was in any danger. But a few years after our divorce and about six months after the American Film Institute honored him with a star-studded tribute celebrating his contribution to the film industry, my ex-husband shot and killed his new wife and then killed himself. He had been on my doorstep, threatening me, only two weeks before.

When a national magazine wrote about Jerry the following year and included a brief account of our marriage, my secret was suddenly out of the closet. Friends would say to me, "I never knew. You don't look like a battered woman." I agreed. I didn't think of myself as a battered woman. But then, what did a "battered woman" look like? I started studying the faces where I had been volunteering at a domestic violence shelter, looking for the answer to that question. What I saw were the faces of my neighbors, my mother, my sister, my daughter. I saw myself. The truth is, battered women are all around us. We just don't recognize them, because they look like us. And so I began this journey with my camera to explore the "face" of domestic violence.

PATTY

It's not just some stranger walking up to you on the street and popping you in the head. When it's somebody you make love to every night, who's treated you like a queen, who loves you to death, and you share every part of your being with him, and that person turns around and hits you, it's the most shocking thing. And you know you have to go, logically, but you know that when it's good he makes you feel beautiful, and you love him. So you stay, *you just want things to be normal*. And then he hurts you again, and it starts tearing you apart bit by bit by bit. He tells you how stupid you are and then when you confide in a friend they tell you how stupid you are for staying, and every time you go back to him you hate yourself a little more.

I was young, I was nineteen when it started, the crazy jealousy. Every time I went somewhere to get away, he'd find me. Then he'd fall apart, full of apologies. And I'd go back, I missed him, I missed that obsessive love. I'm twenty-seven now and I'm just beginning to realize that my whole adult life has been a chain reaction to that relationship, that fear. It takes away your ability to trust, it takes away your innocence.

Looking back, she remembers thinking his possessiveness was romantic.

JOANNE

He had a drinking problem, but he said he wanted to get sober. And I believed once he'd stop drinking, he'd stop abusing me and we'd have a great life together. I didn't understand that they were separate issues. When I gave birth to our daughter, he wasn't working, but I'd be the one to get up with her in the night, and when she was colicky, he'd get crazy. I'd be running down the street with my baby in my arms to wake up the nearest neighbor and call my parents to come and get me. And then I'd still have to get up in the morning and go to work. Over and over and over. I moved out a couple of times. But he would make these promises, and I really wanted to keep our family together.

It kept getting worse, but I just didn't know how to get out. Finally one night after he had beaten me up, I knew I couldn't take it anymore. I waited for him to fall asleep, and at two o'clock in the morning, in sweatpants and a nightgown, I tiptoed out of our condo with a quarter in my hand, walked three blocks down the street to a pay phone and called the police. It wasn't over, but it was the first step. He still called, he threatened, he broke in. But I had changed, by then I had a restraining order, and when he violated it, he lost all contact rights. I'm angry at myself that I didn't wake up sooner. Why didn't I leave and stay gone? Why did I keep coming back? I know the answers, but it still doesn't make sense to me.

Joining a women's support group has helped her restore her self-esteem.

DENISE

We were married thirteen years. His friends would always tell him, "Gee, you're so lucky, you've got an attractive woman, and she's so smart, she's so creative, she knows how to take care of a household, you've got it all!" But to him, he always felt he had to compete with me. I had an excellent job, and I'd have to lie all the time about why I missed a flight, why I was late to a meeting. How could I say my intelligent, successful husband hid my distributor cap, or locked me out of the house in the middle of the night so I couldn't get my clothes? Once I'd been working diligently on a presentation that would create an opportunity for me to rise above what he thought I could do. And sure enough, he beat me up that morning. So I walk into work completely disoriented, wearing something not quite appropriate, and I'm standing there having to sell people on my idea. And all I could think about was I just got beat up and I'm feeling all crazy.

She had hoped her professional success would make her husband proud of her.

YOSHI

His favorite place was the bathroom, lecturing me, degrading me for hours. I'd be stuck in the bathroom all night long, terrified, wanting to get out. But I could not escape, I am so small. My brain would get numb, I would think, "He's right, something's wrong with me," and I'd say "I'm sorry." As soon as I agreed with him, he'd be so nice. The honeymoon time. And then it would start over. I got hurt many times.

The police gave me a card with the number of a shelter. I was still married to him when I first knocked on that shelter door. I didn't know what was going on, I didn't have anyone in this country. I needed help but I was so scared to tell anyone. So I went to ask what I should do. I thought it was only me, it only happened in my house. At the shelter they told me it wasn't my fault, and they told me about the cycle of violence. The pattern was exactly the same for me. And then in a group session, each woman there was talking the same story, the same situations, the same pain. I kept thinking, they're talking about *him*. I wasn't alone any longer. I felt so alone for so long when I was with my husband. It's ironic, now that I am alone for the first time in my life, I don't feel lonely at all. It feels good to be independent.

When she was growing up in Japan, girls were encouraged to marry young and be obedient wives.

SANDRA

We were married in El Paso in the 1950s. My ex-husband and his family were very well known there, and he started to go into politics, running for alderman, for city council. He won them all. And every time I called the police, they would come to the house and they would recognize my husband from the papers, or they had gone to high school with him. So they wouldn't arrest him. He would be so cool and calm, and I would be ranting and raving and hysterical. And so they would believe him, nobody believed me.

I don't think I ever would have left of my own free will if it had not been that my oldest daughter started getting sick. The pediatrician asked me, "What's going on at home?" I said, "Nothing." And he said, "She's seven years old, Sandra. Why does she have an ulcer?" My daughter had seen a lot of violence. She saw her father throw a steak knife at me and it hit the house-keeper. She had seen him throw food on the ceiling. She remembers hiding in her room, when we would push the dressers against the door. Or sleeping in my little red Volkswagon, all five of us, the two little ones in the cubby hole by the back window. They all saw it when he broke my nose. So the doctor kept pushing, "What's going on?" Finally I said it, "My husband is hurting me." I left his office, and it dawned on me, I'm doing the same thing to my kids that my mother did to me. I went down the next day, got a lawyer and filed for divorce.

Like most young wives in the 1950s, her dream was to make a nice home for her family.

DORIS

I ask myself, "Has it always been this way?" Why didn't I know about it until it happened to me? I knew there were women that were beaten, but I thought it was a rare occurrence and only happened to so called low-class people. I certainly never thought it happened to women like me. I was financially independent and owned my own home when I met Bob. And actually, he could have been from any background, and I don't feel that any amount of money or education would have made him any different.

She was convicted of manslaughter for the death of her abusive husband.

BERNITA

He was and still is an investigator with the police department, and I worked with the sheriff's department, undercover in a special unit. During the first year of our relationship there were indications that he was abusive. I didn't like some of the things he said, and how he said them to me. But I made excuses for him. There is so much stress that a police officer experiences on the streets, and then there are all the pressures of just being a black man in America. As an educated African-American woman you're socialized to support your man in the areas where he's really feeling down and suppressed, and encourage him in areas you feel he has potential. And so I went into my nurturing mode.

But his anger escalated. I hadn't seen this at home, it was all new to me. Looking at another man walking down the street would be cause for me to suffer pain. Going against him in a conversation with other people would be cause for me to suffer pain. I found myself having sex with him to keep from getting hit, to keep from getting raped. And the violent times, I prayed. I didn't end it because I thought he would hurt me. I didn't file a police report because I believed it would humiliate him in the department or cause him to lose his position, and that would put me at greater risk. My partner at work was the only one who knew, but after the first episode she said to me, "He only hit you once, and look at how much he has going for him, he's a great catch." Finally I decided that if I was going to die because of this relationship, I would die getting out of it and not staying in it.

After she left him, she co-founded a battered women's shelter in an inner-city neighborhood.

Jane

I met him when I was fourteen and we finally got together ten years later. He was so refreshingly funny and positive. I loved him, he was my mentor, he was my best friend. When he started telling me what to do and what to think, I didn't see it as a control issue, I just thought it was his way of telling me to take care of myself. After we were married, our relationship went from "You're amazing, Jane," to "You're worthless." In the beginning I just kept trying to make it better. And then towards the end it was like waiting for a pat on the head. He had me reduced to a child, I was so brainwashed. I think it was the repetitiveness of hearing how stupid and useless I was, that I was never good enough. What I thought didn't matter, what I wanted wasn't important, I was never right, I was always wrong. Over trivial things, a misplaced milk cap, canned gravy, the night-light. He kept saying this to me over and over and over. To the point where, towards the end, I really believed there was something wrong with me, that he must be right, I couldn't function in the outside world without him. I just stayed at home, my whole life revolved around him walking through the front door. It was as though I had lost my personhood.

She finally realized that trying harder to please him wouldn't change his behavior.

CONNIE

My mother had always said I had such a sassy mouth that someday somebody was bound to knock my front teeth down my throat. So when he'd slap me, I thought I was getting my comeuppance. I had everything: a beautiful BMW in the garage, fur coats, my groceries delivered to me from fancy stores. When I told my mother what was happening, she didn't want to hear about the abuse, because he was supporting her, too. It got progressively worse and worse. He would lock me in the house, where I couldn't get out and he'd take the telephones away. And he told me, "If you try to go out that window I will kill you and I will kill your child." I stayed because I believed him.

My son says he doesn't remember much of it, but I feel it had a big influence on him. For a while he displayed a lot of hostility towards me, sometimes in a passive way and sometimes more aggressively. Even though he knows better, I think he's subconsciously angry with me for walking away from the financial security and forcing him to spend the second half of his childhood being so poor, with me working two jobs to support us.

She knew her decision to leave would mean financial hardship.

BEATRIZ

I never told anybody. In my culture, you keep these things to yourself. If you get married then it's for life, and you have to take whatever is dished out to you. We were married for twenty-four years. The ugliest for me was when it carried over into our intimate life, I was just something he owned and could use at will, and kick aside when he was done. I knew it wasn't right, but I was afraid to say anything to anybody because he was so well liked in the community. I was afraid they would say, "Oh, him? You must be crazy, he is *so* nice." Everyone that knows him only knows him from the outside; he goes out of his way to be good to people—except with us at home. But he was great at making up, always the trips to Mexico, Hawaii, coming home with roses, with jewelry, telling me he'd be better, that he loved me, that he couldn't live without me. Everyone kept telling me how lucky I was to have a man like him, he was so good to us.

When I told the kids I had finally made a decision and had filed for divorce, they said, "Why didn't you do it sooner? Why did you wait so long?" I ask myself the same question.

Her first step to a new life was breaking the silence about the abuse.

MARY

I didn't want to verbalize what was happening to me because that would make it real. The transformation you go through is so subtle, and it's so progressive. I'm sure every girl when they're a teenager says, "No man will ever hit me!" And then, when it happens to you, you rationalize it and justify it, because you don't want it to be so. What are you going to do if you've made a commitment to this man, this relationship, this life, and it isn't what you thought it would be? You can't reason with somebody about this when they say, "Well, you can just leave . . . " The thing is, you're so cut off from the real world. I guess I had never honestly thought of myself as a battered woman. I thought of myself as not having the best marriage.

When I was arrested, there was so much I was going through, so many issues that came up. I mean, this is the man, even though you were terrified of him, part of you hated him, another part of you worshipped the ground he walked on. And here you had, in one fell swoop, killed him and destroyed your entire life. There was so much shame and guilt and of course you have no self-esteem anyway. And then the state comes in, and they make you ashamed for saving your own life. How is it a crime to save your own life?

She was acquitted in 1983 after killing her abusive husband in self-defense.

CHRISTY

I got married when I was fourteen years old, had my first baby at fifteen, the second at seventeen. My husband abused me for six and a half years, but I had two babies and no job skills and I felt trapped. I tried hard to maintain my home so that my own children could have the stability I didn't have growing up in foster homes. But now my children are being raised by the mother of the man who abused me.

All of my dreams faded with the reality of a violent relationship reaching that fatal point. And then they threw my life away in court. After I was convicted I made a resolution to learn the law and find out how this could have happened. I earned my paralegal certificate and worked as a law clerk at the prison library for two years. Now I'm working on a writ and hope to get a new trial. I'll never stop trying.

She is serving 16 years to life in prison for killing her husband while he was battering her.

VALL

I had just moved to California, gotten my first job as an engineer, and this was my first real relationship. I was young, I thought I was in love. It started out normal enough for the first six months. The first incident I vividly recall, we had had an argument, and I started to go up the stairs and the next thing I knew I was flat on my back at the bottom of the stairs. It took me a minute to even realize what happened. She had run up behind me and grabbed the collar of my robe, and just pulled. After that there was little incident after little incident.

Friends were telling me this wasn't healthy, but I would justify it, saying, "Well, this is the woman I love, this is the woman I want to spend the rest of my life with." And so I stayed. My arm is still scarred from her biting me, and from when she threw a knife at me from across the room. She would get angry and just start going off. And then she would call the police and say I attacked her. If you put the two of us side by side, you'd swear I was the one that must be abusing her, because she was a lot smaller. She would say, "I'm sorry, I didn't mean to do it. You bring out the worst in me, that's why I do the things I do. Obviously I must love you, I care enough about you to get that angry." For a long time, I believed that, I thought it must be me. I didn't realize that it was about her, not me, and that trying harder or loving her more would not solve the problem.

She thought that battering only happened in heterosexual relationships.

ROSEMARY

We had started out ten years earlier with dreams of
marriage and family, very much in love. He was the
successful professional, I was the artist, the loving wife. I
felt lucky that his income allowed me to stay home and
raise a child, but during my pregnancy his anger began
to accelerate. I never knew when he walked in the door
whether we would have a pleasant family evening or if it
would be horrible. He kept making excuses for his
behavior, and I kept listening. For years he would flip
out without provocation and start throwing objects
around in fits of rage. It would scare the daylights out of
me, and it would scare my son, he'd wake up crying. I
didn't understand, and I tried harder to make the
marriage work. But as his anger turned to violence, I
became confused. And then eventually it was me he was
throwing around. Finally, after the most severe assault, I
had a glimpse of myself in the mirror. It was a shock.
There were bruises all over my body, my lip was
swollen, black and blue. I had to admit to myself what
was happening to me. When I first went to the lawyer, I
was so ashamed, I could only whisper it, "He's been
hurting me."

*Now divorced, she still has to see him at their
son's soccer games.*

GLENDA

I couldn't understand the nightmare it became. But when the man you love puts his head in your lap and cries and tells you how sorry he is, that he didn't mean to do it, you want to believe it will change. That's what love's supposed to be about, isn't it?

My daughter said, "Mom, you've got to get out of there because he's going to kill you one of these days, and then I won't have you anymore." And I knew she was right. But it was my decision to leave that precipitated his rage and caused the final, fatal incident. And here I sit, and my daughter still doesn't have me.

After turning down a plea bargain, sure she would never be convicted for self-defense, she was sentenced to 17 years to life in prison.

LINDA

They give you a box of Kleenex and a questionnaire, with questions like "How many times were you beaten?" and "Look back and what's the first sign that kind of told you?" And it's very difficult to think back to what it was like. I remember in the beginning when my husband would question me after I had been to the grocery store: "Why did it take you so long? Did you talk to anyone?" But I thought it was wonderful at the time, here's a guy that really cares about me.

The first time it got out of control, he started crying and said, "I am so sorry, it'll never happen again." And that was the start of it, it never did finish after that.

I would get up to go to work at 5:30, and I would wake up before the alarm, I was so afraid of waking him, and I would know just where to go in the dark. I would silently put on my makeup, and my biggest fear would be if I saw his nightstand light go on. I can't tell you how it felt to see it go on. My heart, my whole body, would tremble, watching to see if that light would come on. Do you know how many times I'd have to call in sick?

You don't even think at the time about what you could do. Where was I going to go? I couldn't go to a shelter because they wouldn't take my dog. I've had this dog for thirteen years, and I wasn't going to leave her. So I felt that I had nowhere to go, I felt trapped. When I finally reached the breaking point where I saw my kids suffering and I was willing to die to get away, how I finally did it is, I made a plan and I kept focused on that plan. I got help from unexpected places, like the parents of my daughter's school friend. But people think you can just leave and it's over, and it doesn't work like that. For the next two years after I left him, he terrorized us, he stalked me, he broke in, he tried to poison the dog, the police were always being called. There doesn't seem to be any easy answer.

Granted a lifetime restraining order, she is building a new life for herself and her children.

DIANE

I got out twenty years ago, and in those days no one talked about things like abuse. I didn't tell one person in my life what was going on. After I left, I was very bitter for many years, I didn't go out with any men, I didn't have any social life. My therapy was just hard work and taking care of my kids. I really didn't think about it until ten years later, when I heard from a friend about a women's shelter. It was like a light bulb went off in my head. I knew I had to get involved. When I was taking the shelter training to work on the hot line, I learned the prototype of a batterer, and I could look back and see the characteristics in my ex-husband. And there's a prototype of a victim, and I could see that I was sort of that type, very nurturing and traditional, always willing to take blame myself rather than blame someone else. I've learned so much, it's changed me dramatically.

Through the shelter I learned of a growing movement to help women incarcerated for killing their abusive husbands and I volunteered to work on a clemency petition. The prisoner I interviewed had been battered for thirty-one years. She couldn't even look us in the eye, she was so embarrassed, and still blaming herself for being abused. Her words took me back. It's one of the reasons I'm so involved now, there isn't anything anyone could say to me that I haven't either experienced myself or that I don't understand, as far as why women stay, why they keep it a secret. And since I've been through it I can help.

She and her grown children have a loving and supportive relationship with her second husband.

GENEVIEVE

People always ask, "Why didn't you leave?" Some
women have just been conditioned. That's all I ever saw
growing up, battering and abuse. So that's what you
think a relationship or family *is*. We didn't have a name
for it, we always knew it wasn't right, but you didn't talk
about it then.

*She is currently serving a sentence of 17 years
to life for killing her batterer.*

JAE

He was a "nice Jewish boy" and as a single mother, having someone so eager to be a real dad for my son was attractive. It especially sounded good to me because it sounded good to my family; it was important to make my life acceptable to them. But it wasn't long before we started having problems and went into counseling. Sitting there with my husband, I didn't have the comfort level to explain what was really happening. The therapist said, "He's going a little overboard on the discipline with your son because you keep stepping in the way, you're overly protective, just back off, and don't undermine his discipline in front of the child." I respected this woman, but doing what she said sent a message to my son that my husband's mistreatment was OK with me. And whenever I tried jumping into the middle to stop the assaults, it only enraged the situation. I felt so isolated and confused, and every time he raised a hand to my kid, I became dead inside, much deader than when the abuse was directed at me. Looking back on it, I feel sick. I can't explain how it could have gone on for years.

In 1986 I saw a television talk show about the effects of child abuse, and it just clicked. I got my son out of the house that same night, though I didn't know at the time we were leaving for good. We went to my parents for support, but they felt uncomfortable talking about something so unpleasant, and I finally spoke to a volunteer at the synagogue crisis center. I was very guarded, afraid that if I said what had happened to my son, my allowing it would be considered a crime. And this woman, in the kindest possible way, said to me, "I think you're a battered woman. And I won't feel comfortable if you leave here without calling a shelter hot line, can we do that?" At first I felt mortified, sure that I had over-dramatized the situation, this didn't happen in Jewish families. Finally, it was a relief to discover that what I was suffering silently had an explanation, and a name, and a course of action, and a safe place I could go to deal with it.

She didn't think things like this happened in Jewish families.

JEANETTE AND MICHELLE

Jeanette: I'm working on getting a bond again between my mom and me, we're still not that close yet, because I was so young when everything happened. The hardest thing was when we found out that she wasn't ever coming home, it felt like she abandoned us. I still don't understand how her sentence could be so long.

Michelle: I only remember my father in my dreams. All of my memories of him are him and my mom fighting, or of being afraid when he came home. I don't have any good memories of my father. I just remember him always mad at her, and my mom always getting hit. He'd come after me with a belt and I was barely three or four, and my mom would step in try to stop him, and then she would get beat. That's all the memories I have of growing up.

Their mother is serving a sentence of life in prison without the possibility of parole for the death of their father.

BARBARA

The abuse started almost immediately after we were married. It was like we got married and now he had me and could do what he wanted to me. The first time, I guess I was in shock, I didn't believe it had happened. He never apologized, never mentioned it. And that was just the beginning. I was really ashamed of what was going on, I was afraid of anybody finding out, and still not really believing it was happening to me and always thinking it wasn't going to happen any more. I thought I was the only one, the only one in the world this happened to. After awhile you see yourself through your batterer's eyes and it's not a pretty thing to look at. He made me believe it was my fault, that there was something wrong with me, that I couldn't give enough or be enough to make my marriage work. I don't know how it happened but he convinced me of that.

After all these years on my own, I'm only just beginning to feel like a whole person again. I got angry at something the other day, and it felt good. I was so afraid to express myself for so long. I was never able to say to him, "That was wrong, you did a bad thing, you destroyed a life." I could say it now.

After her divorce, counseling helped her regain her confidence.

AMINAH

My husband had beaten me for ten years and once burned my face with an electrical hair-straightening comb. I can still close my eyes and remember that feeling, the fear, the isolation. I just didn't want to be hurt anymore. I got life without possibility of parole. The judge told me that twenty-four hours after I'm dead, I could be released. And so I started clipping out newspaper articles about people who had done really horrible crimes and how much less of a sentence they received. And I started writing letters back in 1978 or '79. I did it completely on my own, there weren't any advocate groups then. Finally I had generated so much public support that the governor had to listen to my story. It took me sixteen years to do it, but he granted me clemency.

I hadn't had Christmas with my children for sixteen years, I hadn't driven a car, it was like starting a whole new life. But even after so many years, I still have lingering fears left over from those days when I was a battered woman, like I'm terrified to drive at night. People who haven't experienced it themselves just don't understand what it does to you. I decided to put my own experiences to some constructive use, and I'm working at a women's shelter now.

She was granted clemency by the governor of Iowa after serving 16 years in prison.

KIMBERLY

We met in college, in my radical liberal days. He was
the only man I'd ever slept with, so I didn't know how it
was supposed to be. It was never gentle, he never held
me. He'd twist me around and hurt me and when he was
done with me he'd go take a shower. But I'm very
traditional, and in my religion, sleeping with a man was
making a commitment to spend your life together, and I
took that seriously.

For a long time I thought things would change, and of
course they never did. Finally I couldn't live with the
psychotic behavior anymore. I thought leaving him
would end the problem, and so I had a girlfriend help
me secretly move all of my things out of our storage
unit. The next day when he found out what I had done,
he got crazy and violent and a neighbor called the
police. Which was good, they got him out, got me an
emergency protective order and took me to the hospital.
But it wasn't over, it was only the beginning. He just
wouldn't let go. I lived with terror for so long that when
my apartment caved in around me during the earthquake, I wasn't that scared. At least with the earthquake
I could understand what was happening and why. With
my boyfriend none of it ever made any sense.

She still believes there are many good men out
there who are capable of having healthy,
loving relationships.

PEGGIE

I got married at sixteen, and when my husband blacked my eye three days after the wedding, our minister told me I needed to learn to be a better wife and not talk back. I had no one to tell me it wasn't right, that it didn't have to be that way. So I tried to be a better wife and stayed with him for twelve years.

Five years later I married again, to a person I thought was very different. He was very soft-spoken, took us hiking and camping, and seemed to represent the kind of wholesome life I had always yearned for, a safe haven for myself and my daughters. I know now that there were signs from the beginning, but I certainly didn't have the knowledge to identify them. I don't remember exactly what happened; I do remember his motorcycle boot connecting with my face. I woke up in the hospital, with doctors and nurses and lights everywhere. But there wasn't any sound. I didn't hear any sounds again for two and a half years. I had to go to school to learn to sign, and to learn the deaf culture. My entire life changed because of what he had done to me. But my husband only went to jail for four hours. And he kept harassing me until I moved out of the area and he no longer knew where to find me.

When I graduated from college in 1980, I decided to turn what had happened to me into something constructive and began teaching self-defense classes and creating community support groups for deaf abuse victims. Just imagine the isolation a battered woman must feel when she can't communicate with spoken words. I knew I could help.

She continues to advocate for deaf and disabled women.

CATHERINE

My family is very Catholic. You get married and you stay married for life. I was sixteen when I met Tom, eighteen when we got married. Six months later my first baby was born and four months after that I was pregnant again. Tom joined the police force that year. We didn't have money, I didn't have a car, I was stuck in the house, I was lonely. By the time I was twenty-six I knew I didn't want to be with him anymore, but I had four babies to take care of. What do you do?

I finished school and got on the police department in 1989. In January of 1990, when I told Tom I wanted a divorce, he locked himself in the bathroom and said he was going to shoot himself. From then on, any time I would try to bring up the idea of leaving him, he would get angry and violent and suicidal. You get scared and so you don't talk about it. The more I emotionally separated from him, the more he'd close in on me, he wouldn't leave me alone. He would look up the location of my black and white on the computer, he would follow me on radio calls. Or he'd call me at work and tell me he didn't want to live anymore, and he'd be at home with our kids, and I would panic that they were in danger. In December of 1990, I was in the room with my two-year-old daughter, and he threw a photograph of us on the floor, took out his gun and shot it. When the psychologist I was seeing found out about this incident, she felt I was in danger and reported it to the department. But by not having reported it myself, when it happened, I had committed felony child endangerment. So my job was threatened, I had to take a two-day suspension without pay, I got punished for what he did. I hadn't reported it because I was so afraid of what he'd do, but no one seemed to understand. My family said I should just try and make my marriage work. I felt I had no support anywhere, and I felt completely alone.

When her father disapproved of her decision to leave her husband, she found support elsewhere.

ESTERLINA

I met him at a church garage sale. I had been a missionary in the Philippines so it's my natural instinct to reach out, and his stories about childhood family rejection and reform school made me feel compassionate. He proposed to me right away, and I became pregnant as soon as we were married. It was amazing how immediately he changed, he became so angry. He would call me names but that didn't affect me so much, because they were English words and I didn't really understand them so well. But it didn't stop at words. After the first time he hurt me, he promised me it wouldn't happen again and he agreed to get counseling. Then he only went one time, and after one month it started again, so much rage. And that's when I left him.

I went to a women's shelter, and I was awakened, because I got to talk to other women. I realized there are many stories worse than mine, many more years of pain, but the cycle is the same. And even though all the stories are different, they are also all the same.

It hurts to think the violence will come back, I still want to believe he will get cured. He wrote me a touching letter, he wants us to be together. Sometimes I feel, "Oh, poor man, he needs my help. My love can heal him." I know now that it's not my problem to fix, it's his problem. But I feel the need to keep going to the support group, it helps me stay strong. And I don't want to be tempted to go back.

It still helps her to share her story with other women in a group.

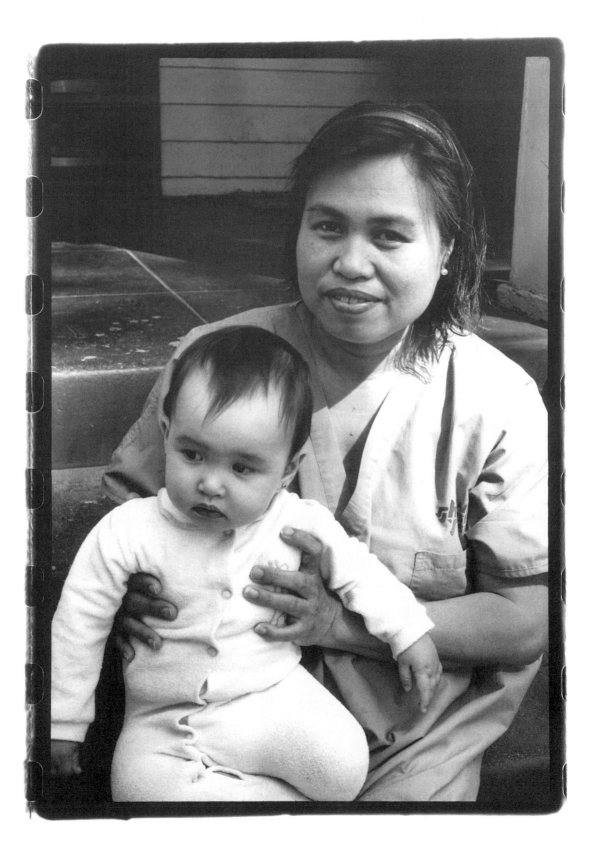

JO ANN

We were married seventeen years. He wasn't from the projects like I was, and I saw him as this good person who was better than me. He started working for the IRS, he was making good money, we had everything we wanted. But I had no self-esteem, when somebody is constantly telling you that you're ugly, that you're nothing. I didn't have friends, I couldn't have friends, I couldn't go out. When I finally got a job he would follow me to work, he didn't believe where I was going. He started getting abusive with the kids, and one day I just looked at my children's faces, and I couldn't take it anymore. They had seen so much violence, it breaks my heart. So that day, we weren't fighting, I wasn't mad, I just looked at their faces and knew it had to come to an end. I got up and told him to leave. And he did, that was the last time he lived here.

He stalked me for years after he left, I'm talking major stalking. He would get on the roof of my house, cut my electricity off, cut my phone lines. He put gasoline on my front lawn. He super-glued all my doors locked. The police were always at my door. The last time he was arrested he pleaded guilty to fifteen counts. It's been hard for my kids. But we survived it, you know.

After her divorce became final, she changed
54 | *her name and took a job in another state.*

DANIEL

It was July 1st when my dad broke my mom's leg. My dad was here on a visitation with my little brother. I was playing a video game when I heard my mom start screaming, it was a terrible scream and I was so scared. I ran in and tried to stop him. Then my mom told me to call 911. While I was on the telephone to 911 my grandfather, he's about eighty-seven I think, he hobbled over and tried to stop my dad, but my dad hit him in the face. I tried to stop him again and then he punched me about five or six times. I had these big bruises on my face, and I had to go to the hospital later because I kept getting dizzy spells and bloody noses. I feel more than hate. I never want to see my dad. And I don't have to because the court said it's not safe for me. But the court said my brother has to see my dad. I don't understand, if it's not safe for me, how can it be safe for a little baby?

Nine years old, he worries about his toddler brother.

PATRICIA

I grew up in a sheltered, upper middle class environment and married a boy I grew up with. It wasn't that we didn't love each other, but we were more like siblings, and after eight years we parted as friends. I always knew there was a passion missing, so two or three years after my divorce, when I met this knight in shining armor, I was completely swept away. He was charming, romantic, incredibly passionate, and he was madly in love with me, all these things I had never experienced from a man. Looking back, there were signs from the beginning, some hard edges. But I was really attracted to that rebel personification. After we were married, I kept making excuses for his anger and thinking it was me. Because if it was me then I had some control over it, I could change it. I thought about getting out, but it had gotten to the point where I couldn't get my feet on the ground, he had broken my eardrum and fractured my jaw, I was so disoriented. I thought this just didn't happen to people in my class.

What finally shifted was that my grandmother, who I was really close to, had a heart attack. We had had some conflict because she wanted me to get out of this relationship, but I thought it was just her snobbish conservative ways. Now she was in the hospital, and she said to me, "I'm afraid he's going to kill you, you have to believe me," and then she died a few hours later. When my husband picked me up from the airport the next day, he was angry that I had left him to go to her, and he got really violent. I kept hearing my grandmother's words, and the next morning I quietly told my daughter to go get in the car. I took almost nothing, and I just started driving north. I didn't even call my mom, I was afraid if they knew anything it would somehow endanger them. I ended up about four hours away, at a friend of my father's who was a lawyer. I filed my divorce from there.

Even though she now feels safe, she still lives in a security building with no name on the mailbox.

LINDA R.

I was ignorant of the evolving abuse in my seven-year, live-in relationship with Ron. It progressed so slowly, I just became accustomed to the ridicule, the condemnation, the constant mistreatment and verbal assaults. Common public humiliations routinely ended in silent rides home. I recall vividly the searing pain of rejection, of feeling inferior, unwanted, and incredibly isolated, constantly stifling my emotions to avoid conflict, fearing the loss of his love.

Retracing the relationship in my mind a million times, searching for understanding of this insanity, I see clearly that I had always glossed over his abusiveness towards me to salvage the love. Even when he struck me in the face in public or slammed me up against the fireplace mantle, I failed to recognize the potential for greater harm. And I had never had any reason or experience to cause me to really fear anyone, before that exact moment when Ron threatened my life and I knew he meant it. One moment. Our perpetual psychological and emotional roller coaster ride ended in my suicide attempt, and Ron's death.

She is now serving 27 years to life in prison for killing her abuser.

NARIA

I always had to reassure him how much I cared for him, but he would never say he loved me, he was always afraid to show too much of himself. I saw him as a scared little boy and it touched this motherly thing in me, that's what kept me in the relationship for so long.

When it started to get ugly, I tried to break it off many times. But he would always try to control me. He would push me, grab me, lock me out, he would spit on me. We were teachers at the same school, and one summer while he was away as a camp guide, I moved all of my things out of the house and went to my mother's. He came there and gave me his big sad story about why I should come back. I moved into a new apartment, and he found me again. When he stopped by on Christmas day, I told him that I didn't feel comfortable with him being there and asked him to leave. He came after me, grabbed me and twisted me, and I fell against the railing, cracking my head open. He took me to the emergency room and then stood by me so I couldn't tell the nurse what really happened. But finally he had to make a phone call about my insurance, and while he was gone I told her, "He did this to me." And she called the police.

Not wanting to live the rest of her life in fear, she changed her name and moved out of the country.

MARION

Because of one moment in time, my life is forever changed. My friend's life is gone, and I do wish I could change that, but it was an accident and no amount of time that I serve will bring her back. I don't make any excuses for what I've done, but I don't believe the sentence I received was reasonable for the crime when you compare my case to other crimes. I'm glad the public is beginning to learn about battered women's syndrome, understanding abuse for what it is. Maybe justice can be done for others, even if it's too late for me.

My partner was much younger and she sometimes drank and took drugs, and at those times she would get crazy and that's when she would jump on me. One time she and I were fighting because I wouldn't give her any money, and I got knocked down. She kicked me in the side and stomach, took what she could find and left. My grandkids put me in bed where I stayed for three or four days, and finally I was taken to the hospital. I was bleeding internally and they had to remove my spleen. She came to the hospital crying and told me how sorry she was and she would never hurt me again. I was so sick and so glad to see her, and when she kissed me I was in love all over again. She took me home and all was well for a while, but then it started up just like before. The rest is history. Here I sit doing seventeen years to life for second-degree murder. End of story.

Marion died in prison in 1993.

KATHI

I knew him, Mr. Wonderful, for three years before I even dated him, and then I lived with him for eight months. He started being verbally abusive to the point where I got scared and broke off the engagement, but then he started calling me. He was a Southern gentleman and he had all the right things to say. We got back together and went to see his family in Tennessee for Thanksgiving. All of a sudden he started to pressure me to get married, right then and there, even though we had already planned a big wedding for February and I had bought a wedding gown, the whole thing was set. But then he couldn't find a chapel that was open because of the holiday and he got very frustrated. The next morning we got up and as I was bending over getting dressed, he just decked me, right up into the jaw, across the face. No reason for it, no warning whatsoever. I was bleeding and couldn't stop crying, the pain was so violent. I thought he'd broken my jaw, but nothing showed up on the emergency room x-rays. The relationship was over with that one blow, but the pain wouldn't seem to end, and two and a half years later, my face literally collapsed one day at work. What he'd done was crack the upper facial bone that goes right across the top of the nose. I had to have three reconstructive surgeries to repair the damage. But more than your bones, it's your innocence, your trust, your spirit that gets broken. There isn't any surgery to fix that.

Recently married, her husband is patient and
supportive with her lingering fears.

BRENDA

It's not right that I took a life and I'm very sorry for that and I wish I could take it back. But it happened because I feared for my life and I believed I had no other choice. That's the state of mind I was in at that time after being so physically and mentally abused by this man. And now the death of my husband is one more horror I have to live with the rest of my life.

I met Rick when I was sixteen years old. He was good-looking and charming, and he showered me with attention, making me feel beautiful for the first time in my life. I didn't see the warning signs in his possessive behavior; I thought it was cute, I thought it meant he loved me. When he hit me on our wedding day, he cradled me in his arms and begged my forgiveness. His mother said, "It's just the stress of the wedding." And I was a pregnant seventeen-year-old girl, starry-eyed with love and hope for the future. He'd never hurt me again and we'd live happily ever after. And so began a ten-year litany of abuse and pain that was punctuated by the pounding of his fists on my face, my body, my soul. I left with my three daughters several times, but he'd always track us down. By the final year of our marriage, my life had deteriorated into a nightmare of fear, pain and despair, and I didn't know how to help myself.

After serving 10 years for killing her husband, she was released from prison in March 1997, becoming the first woman in California to be granted clemency based on battered woman's syndrome. She is now building a new life with her children and continues to be an outspoken advocate on behalf of other abused women.

It's difficult for someone on the outside to understand the isolation and hopelessness a battered woman feels. Sometimes looking back, it's difficult for me to understand it myself, because I'm in such a different state of mind today. Even when I went to trial, I didn't know I was a battered woman. I didn't realize it until I joined a support group in prison, where I heard other women talk about going through the same experiences.

The most important thing a woman living in an abusive relationship needs to know is, she needs to tell someone what's going on, there is help available, she's not alone.

WHERE TO FIND HELP

National Domestic Violence Hotline
(800) 799-SAFE (7233)
TDD (800) 787-3224

National Resource Center on Domestic
Violence
(800) 537-2238

Resource Center on Domestic Violence,
Child Protection and Custody
(800) 527-3223

Battered Women's Justice Project
206 West Fourth Street
Duluth, MN 55806
(800) 903-0111

Center for the Prevention of Sexual and
Domestic Violence
1914 North 34th Street, Suite 105
Seattle, WA 98103
(206) 634-1903

Domestic Abuse Awareness Project
P.O. Box 1155
Madison Square Station
New York, NY 10159-1155
(212) 353-1755
(212) 353-8645 fax

Domestic Abuse Project
204 West Franklin Avenue
Minneapolis, MN 55404
(612) 874-7063

Family Violence Prevention Fund
38 Rhode Island Street, Suite 304
San Francisco, CA 94103-5133
(415) 252-8900

Gay and Lesbian Anti-Violence Project
647 Hudson Street
New York, NY 10014
(212) 807-0197

National Coalition Against Domestic
Violence (NCADV)
National Office
P.O. Box 18749
Denver, CO 80218-0749
(303) 839-1852

National Council on Child Abuse and
Family Violence
1155 Connecticut Avenue NW, Suite 400
Washington, DC 20036
(800) 222-2000
(202) 429-6695

National Victim Center
309 West 7th Street, Suite 705
Fort Worth, TX 76102
(800) FYI-CALL
Provides information and referrals, not crisis
counseling.

National Battered Women's Law Project
at the National Center on Women and
Family Law
799 Broadway, Suite 402
New York, NY 10003
(212) 674-8200

National Clearinghouse for the Defense of
Battered Women
125 South 9th Street, Suite 302
Philadelphia, PA 19107
(215) 351-0010
Provides resources for defending women
charged with crimes, including killing their
abuser.

Sojourn Services for Battered Women and
Their Children
P.O. Box 5597
Santa Monica, CA 90409
(310) 392-9896, 24-hour hot line

WOMAN, Inc.
333 Valencia Street, Suite 251
San Francisco, CA 94103
(415) 864-4722
For lesbians in violent relationships.

Women of Color Task Force Against
Domestic Violence
P.O. Box 1743
Aurora, CO 80040
(303) 696-9196

SUGGESTED READING

The Battered Woman's Survival Guide: Breaking the Cycle by Jan Berliner Statman, Dallas: Taylor Publishing, 1995.

Before It's Too Late: Helping Women in Controlling or Abusive Relationships by Robert J. Ackerman and Susan E. Pickering, Deerfield Beach, FL: Health Communications, Inc., 1995.

Chain Chain Change: For Black Women in Abusive Relationships by Evelyn C. White, Seattle: Seal Press, 1994.

A Community Secret: For the Filipina in an Abusive Relationship by Jacqueline Agtuca, Seattle: Seal Press, 1994.

Dating Violence: Young Women in Danger edited by Barrie Levy, Seattle: Seal Press, 1991.

Defending Our Lives: Getting Away from Domestic Violence and Staying Safe by Susan Murphy-Milano, New York: Anchor Books, 1996.

The Domestic Violence Sourcebook by Dawn Bradley Berry, Los Angeles: Lowell House, 1995.

The Emotionally Abused Woman: Overcoming Destructive Patterns and Reclaiming Yourself by Beverly Engel, New York: Fawcett Columbine, 1990.

Encouragements for the Emotionally Abused Woman: Wisdom and Hope for Women at Any Stage of Emotional Abuse Recovery by Beverly Engel, New York: Fawcett Columbine, 1993.

Getting Free: You Can End Abuse and Take Back Your Life by Ginny NiCarthy, Seattle: Seal Press, 1997.

Getting Up When You're Feeling Down: A Woman's Guide to Overcoming and Preventing Depression by Harriet Braiker, New York: G.P. Putnam, 1990.

Healing Your Life: Recovery from Domestic Violence by Candace Hennekens, Pro Writing Services and Press, 1991.

In Love and In Danger: A Teen's Guide to Breaking Free of Abusive Relationships by Barrie Levy, Seattle: Seal Press, 1993.

It Could Happen to Anyone: Why Battered Women Stay by Ola W. Barnett and Alyce D. LaViolette, Newbury Park, CA: Sage Publications, 1993.

It's Not Okay Anymore: Your Personal Guide to Ending Abuse, Taking Charge, and Loving Yourself by Greg Enns and Jan Black, Oakland: New Harbinger Publications, 1997.

Mejor Sola Que Mal Acompañada: For the Latina in an Abusive Relationship/ Para la mujer golpeada by Myrna M. Zambrano, Seattle: Seal Press, 1985.

Mommy and Daddy Are Fighting: A Book for Children About Family Violence by Susan Paris, illustrated by Gail Labinski, Seattle: Seal Press, 1986.

Naming the Violence: Speaking Out Against Lesbian Battering, edited by Kerry Lobel, Seattle: Seal Press, 1986.

New Beginnings: A Creative Writing Guide for Women Who Have Left Abusive Partners by Sharon Doane, Seattle: Seal Press, 1996.

The New Our Bodies, Ourselves: A Book by and for Women by The Boston Women's Health Book Collective, Touchstone Books, 1996.

Recovery of Your Self-Esteem: A Guide for Women by Carolyn Hillman, New York: Fireside/Simon & Schuster, 1992.

Revolution from Within: A Book of Self-Esteem by Gloria Steinem, New York: Little, Brown & Company, 1997.

The Single Mother's Companion: Essays and Stories by Women edited by Marsha R. Leslie, Seattle: Seal Press, 1994.

Stop Domestic Violence: An Action Plan for Saving Lives by Lou Brown, Francois Dubau and Merritt McKeon, New York: St. Martin's Press, 1997.

The Verbally Abusive Relationship: How to Recognize It and How to Respond by Patricia Evans, Holbrook, MA: Adams Media Corporation, 1996.

Violent Betrayal: Partner Abuse in Lesbian Relationships by Claire Renzetti, Newbury Park, CA: Sage Publications, 1992.

Violent No More: Helping Men End Domestic Abuse by Michael Payman, Alameda, CA: Hunter House, 1993.

What's a Nice Girl Like You Doing in a Relationship Like This? Women in Abusive Relationships edited by Kay Marie Porterfield, Freedom, CA: The Crossing Press, 1992.

When Battered Women Kill by Angela Browne, New York: Free Press, 1987.

When Love Goes Wrong: What to Do When You Can't Do Anything Right by Ann Jones and Susan Schechter, New York: HarperPerennial, 1992.

The Woman's Comfort Book: A Self-Nurturing Guide for Restoring Balance in Your Life by Jennifer Louden, San Francisco: HarperCollins, 1992.

Women and Male Violence: The Visions and Struggles of the Battered Women's Movement by Susan Schechter, Boston: South End Press, 1982.

You Can Be Free: An Easy-to-Read Handbook for Abused Women by Ginny NiCarthy and Sue Davidson, Seattle: Seal Press, 1997.

Young Men's Work: Building Skills to Stop the Violence: A Ten Session Group Program by Paul Kivel and Alan Creighton, Center City, MN: Hazelden, 1995.

Vera Anderson has been a photojournalist since 1975. She is a recipient of the Barbara Deming Money for Women Award, and her photographic studies about domestic violence have been featured on the *Today Show* and CNN's *World News Tonight.* She is currently the Los Angeles bureau chief of *Cine Premiere* magazine. *A Woman Like You* is her first book.

Notes

Notes

ABOUT SEAL PRESS

Seal Press was founded in 1976 to publish quality books by women writers. Our list includes books on women's health, self-help and recovery, gender studies, parenting, young adult, travel, popular culture, and literary fiction. Since 1982, when we published the first self-help book for battered women, *Getting Free*, we have also been known as one of the country's leading publishers of books about domestic violence. Our publishing goal is to encourage change as well as to inform and enrich the lives of our readers.

If you would like to order a free catalog of our books, please contact us:

Seal Press
3131 Western Avenue, Suite 410
Seattle, Washington 98121-1041
(206) 283-7844 phone / (206) 285-9410 fax
1-800-754-0271 orders only

email: sealprss@scn.org
visit our website: www.sealpress.com